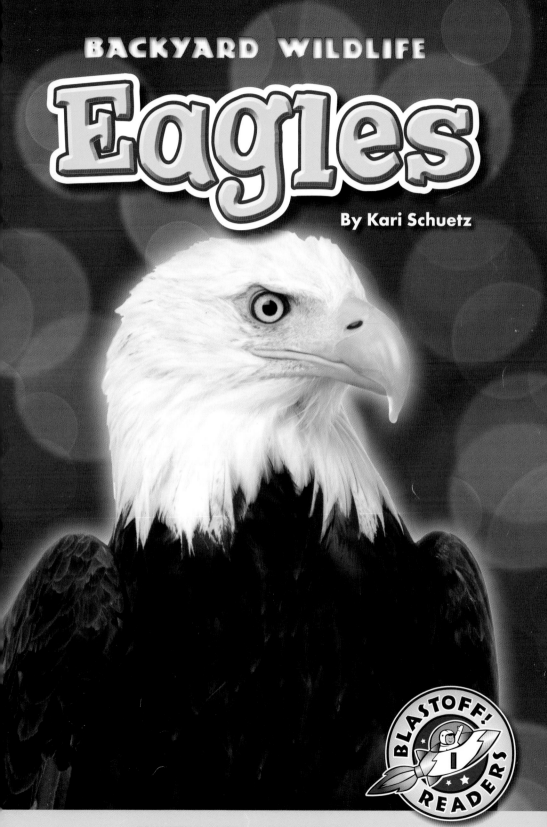

# BACKYARD WILDLIFE

# Eagles

By Kari Schuetz

BELLWETHER MEDIA · MINNEAPOLIS, MN

BLASTOFF! READERS

Note to Librarians, Teachers, and Parents:

**Blastoff! Readers** are carefully developed by literacy experts and combine standards-based content with developmentally appropriate text.

**Level 1** provides the most support through repetition of high-frequency words, light text, predictable sentence patterns, and strong visual support.

**Level 2** offers early readers a bit more challenge through varied simple sentences, increased text load, and less repetition of high-frequency words.

**Level 3** advances early-fluent readers toward fluency through increased text and concept load, less reliance on visuals, longer sentences, and more literary language.

**Level 4** builds reading stamina by providing more text per page, increased use of punctuation, greater variation in sentence patterns, and increasingly challenging vocabulary.

**Level 5** encourages children to move from "learning to read" to "reading to learn" by providing even more text, varied writing styles, and less familiar topics.

Whichever book is right for your reader, Blastoff! Readers are the perfect books to build confidence and encourage a love of reading that will last a lifetime!

This edition first published in 2012 by Bellwether Media, Inc.

No part of this publication may be reproduced in whole or in part without written permission of the publisher. For information regarding permission, write to Bellwether Media, Inc., Attention: Permissions Department, 5357 Penn Avenue South, Minneapolis, MN 55419.

Library of Congress Cataloging-in-Publication Data
Schuetz, Kari.
  Eagles / by Kari Schuetz.
    p. cm. – (Blastoff! readers: backyard wildlife)
  Includes bibliographical references and index.
  Summary: "Developed by literacy experts for students in kindergarten through grade three, this book introduces eagles to young readers through leveled text and related photos"–Provided by publisher.
  ISBN 978-1-60014-721-0 (hardcover : alk. paper)
  1. Eagles–Juvenile literature. I. Title.
  QL696.F32S37 2012
  598.9'42–dc23                                      2011029687

Printed in the United States of America, North Mankato, MN
010112       1207

# Contents

Eagles are **raptors**. Their **wingspan** is at least twice their body length.

Eagles hunt rabbits, snakes, and other small animals. They also snatch fish out of the water.

Eagles use their sharp sight to spot **prey**. They often search for animals from a **perch**.

Eagles swoop down to catch prey. They grab animals with their strong **talons**.

**talons**

Eagles use their talons and hooked **beaks** to tear prey apart.

Eagles build nests in tall trees or high cliffs. Their nests are called **aeries**.

Females lay eggs in their aeries. Males and females sit on the eggs to keep them warm.

Baby eagles are called eaglets. An eaglet uses its **egg tooth** to break through the shell.

egg tooth

Eaglets begin to fly when they are about three months old. Soar, eaglet!

# Glossary

**aeries**—the nests of raptors

**beaks**—the mouths of some animals such as birds and turtles

**egg tooth**—a sharp, hard point of skin on an eaglet's beak

**perch**—a tree branch or other high place where a bird sits

**prey**—animals that are hunted by other animals for food

**raptors**—birds that are skilled hunters; raptors use sharp eyesight, great hearing, and strong talons to hunt prey.

**talons**—sharp nails on the toes of raptors

**wingspan**—the distance between the tips of a bird's wings

# To Learn More

## AT THE LIBRARY

Douglas, Llyod G. *The Bald Eagle.* Chicago, Ill.: Children's Press, 2003.

Goodall, Jane. *The Eagle & the Wren.* New York, N.Y.: North-South Books, 2000.

Price, Anne. *Raptors: The Eagles, Hawks, Falcons, and Owls of North America.* Lanham, Md.: Roberts Rinehart Publishers, 2002.

## ON THE WEB

Learning more about eagles is as easy as 1, 2, 3.

1. Go to www.factsurfer.com.

2. Enter "eagles" into the search box.

3. Click the "Surf" button and you will see a list of related Web sites.

With factsurfer.com, finding more information is just a click away.

# Index

The images in this book are reproduced through the courtesy of: Eric Issellée, front cover; Henry Wilson, pp. 5, 7 (left), 9; Dean Bertoncelj, p. 7 (top); Ra'id Khalil, p. 7 (center); Ilya D. Gridnev, p. 7 (right); Colin Edwards Photography, p. 11; Thomas Sbampato / Photolibrary, p. 13; Aurora Photos / Masterfile, p. 15; Bruce Lichtenberger / Photolibrary, p. 17; Carsten Rehder / Corbis, p. 19; Michael Francis Photography, p. 21.